Rhymes
for Troubled Times

Howard Churchwell

ISBN 978-1-63885-093-9 (Paperback)
ISBN 978-1-63885-094-6 (Digital)

Covenant Books, Inc.
11661 Hwy 707
Murrells Inlet, SC 29576
www.covenantbooks.com

1619

The year of
America's first sin
The bell had rung—the curtain was up and
the atrocities of life were about to begin
Precious cargo from
The eastern
Caribbean Seas
Brought west
With wailing pleas
Cargo bound and chained
In the lower deck
Treated like animals
With no respect
Many died on the
Long journey west
Unable to sleep or eat
And barely had rest
So when these companies
Brag about their earning streams
It all started on the backs of enslaved Africans
In
1619.

A Great Place to Start

Where to begin
With this struggle from within
From the deepest part of life
A light need to be lit
In this dark hollow pit
Filled with negativity and despair
Not standing up
Not giving in
Not giving a care
Shortcomings in me
I wish that I can see
To conceive or believe
The power within
Not filled with sin
As was taught again and again
Genuine faith is what we need
Not to concede
To pain or hardships
Misfortune or sorrow
Putting forth constant effort
Working for a better tomorrow
Standing up and not being shy
Being accountable before we die
With joy and laughter in our heart
Is to be a great place to start.

A Thin Line

Ticktock
Hands on the clock
Keep going and don't stop
Time waits for no man
It's a fact
That can be tracked
Some think we have time
Some believe it's a short line
In fact it keeps going
It's also unknowing
How much time we really have
Some even say
It's infinite in every way
From the beginning to the end
Where does time really begin
A duration
The beginning of a relation
Something fixed
An interval between an action
Within a fraction
Of what may come our way.

An Experience to Share

Difficulties arise
Problems exist
It may come as
A surprise
In the morning mist
Life has its way of
Showing its truth
How we handle it
Comes with couth
Things happen day by day
Night by night
With faith we handle things
Not by sight
We believe in the power of prayer
Handling
Things that we think
We can't bear
But we overcome our
Problems to have
An experience to share.

Anniversary

November 18, 1930, past
Creating value
Would surely last
It was first taught
In education
Then in '44
Taught
Inner transformation
To bring forth
Our highest potential
Of compassion
And wisdom
That is essential
A necessary
Element
For proper
Credentials
November 18
Is a special day.

Blast

Once upon a time there was me wondering if there will ever be

A special someone who would share my life and someday who would be my wife.

Then turned out she was there all along waiting on the sideline waiting for me to complete my song.

We passed each other on many days not knowing that we were meant to be together in any way.

She smiled and I said hello that was the beginning were still together and were still winning.

It's really rare to find that perfect mate but there is nothing rare about believing in fate.

So on this date from twenty years past,

Happy anniversary to my wife, Lori, may we continue to live life to the fullest and to continue to have a blast.

As We Are

Some say that you have to change
or be someone else to be happy
But we need to be who we are at all times
Even if our attitude is sometimes crappy
Life is full of ups and downs
But how we live our lives determines if
our smiles are turned upside down
We study the hope-filled teaching to gather
strength and courage to face life challenges
We chant to become more human
and less like savages
We can be happy in our present form
even in the midst of a winter's storm
So let's light the way for someone else near and far
As we shine our light just as we are.

Be All Right

Stepping into the ring
Ready for the bout
Looking around
Not having any doubts
Determination on your face
Nerves of steel
Keeping a steady pace
Winning at will
Being sure of self
And no one else
We must look deep inside
Putting aside our foolish pride
Everything moving in your favor
Today and not tomorrow or later
Winning is key but it can be
Somewhat of a mystery
Stay focused and keep up the fight
And everything will be all right.

Being True to Oneself

Being true to oneself is like looking in a pond
Looking very close and not from beyond
Seeing a reflection of self as clear as can be
standing as strong as an old oak tree
Seeing ourselves as we are is not an
easy task but by facing our issues with
courage the issues won't surely last
Trust yourself and don't forget
We are more than what we think we are
And we are our best bet yet.

Better Day

Looking around the corner and what do I see
Yesterday how I used to be
Full of sadness with no hope
Unable to handle life unable to cope
Thinking that problems were bigger than my scope
Drinking drowning and smoking dope
Going down a slippery slope
Hitting the bottom really hard
In a drama in which I starred
Played my part to the best that I could
Didn't know life like I thought I should
On the stage of life I performed my act
Lacking substance lacking tact
One day someone showed me how to escape the fray
To work for peace each and every day
How to live my life in an enlightened way
Say these consonants when you bow
Make a wish and make a vow
Nam-myoho-renge-kyo are the words to say
Change your habits
And work for a better day.

Break of Dawn

As the nights grow short
And the days grow long
We rise up with a morning song
Song in our hearts of a new day begins
By challenging ourselves
How were going to win
Win over ourselves helping others
Fathers/sons/daughters/mothers
Showing that there's a better way
To start our morning each and every day
Reflecting what's in our heart
Is a great way to start
With laughter and joy we hope
that happiness will spawn
Again tomorrow
Early at the break of dawn.

Canvass of Your Life

Body is the easel
The frame that stands up tall
Our thoughts and actions
Is the paint that
Prevents us from thinking small
The brush has a careful stroke
Left to right, up and down
So that we can walk with a smile
And not with a frown
The picture that we envision
A portrait hanging on the wall
Our decision not to live in strife
Is to treat life as a ball
We have the potential to create
The reality that we wish
To search thoroughly
As if we were to fish
By turning poison into medicine
We can change the bad to the good
No one else can do it
Only as we have the power that could
So when things go wrong
And it feels like you're being cut by a knife
Take a good look at yourself and
Change the canvass of your life.

Payment Due

Casting off the transient revealing the true
A new day fresh and crisps like the morning dew
Showing our true self to be visible without a rue
The sun over dark clouds come shining through
To see the sky rich with a color of powder blue
To be shown how it's supposed to be without a clue
Not a clever action or accomplishment not a coup
Not a late fee just payment due.

Coming to a Close

Not holding anything back
Looking over the year
Seeing how we attacked
We fought and won
Some we lost
But we did not give up
At any cost
Soka victory
Is winning at every turn
Even when things looked bleak
We chanted with hot determ
Even in losing we have won
Just by not giving up
We still rise and face the morning sun
So let's take the lessons learned
New faith and determination earned
With fresh eyes and new hope
Going up and not down a slope
And looking forward to the new challenges
That we chose
As 2019 comes to a close.

Compassion

Having compassion is not old fashion
and it will never go out of style
That's what the world needs today
even if it's just for a little while
Hating and fighting is not the human way
acting like animals who all ran astray
We must accept our fellow man just as
they are and not judging them to be at
our standards which can be subpar
So when you see someone who looks
sad and down give them a big hello
with a big smile and not a frown
You never know how someone feels
inside they could have lost someone
or someone could have just died
So in this world full of disrespect and full of factions
Let us be the shining example
of love and compassion.

Contribution

To contribute is an act of giving
Freely without misgiving
We contribute our time
If we don't have a dime
Thinking of others
An honorable thing to do
By helping others we help
Ourselves too.
Without looking for any return
Causes that we make
The effects are well earned
To donate is to contribute
In each and every way
Helping others to create happiness
And to have a better day.

Courage, Hope, and Dreams

A smooth sea does not make a skilled sailor
The issues that we face are there to make us greater
A determined mind helps us walk a straight line
First we must master our roaming mind
To seek the skill to live day by day
Is an art to live by rules
Not a game that we play
We must be focused and have a keen eye
An eye on our hopes and dreams before we die
Courage is a must that we manifest
It's a quality that must be professed
We must show and proclaim
Our dignity in life
And not complain
About our problems
Or strife
Be the skilled sailor of life's roaring waves
With hope and courage there are
people that we can Help save
Save them from drowning in their own sea
Life full of misery
Be the example that shines a light
Show them how to handle any plight
With courage hope and dreams
We can handle anything.

Courage

Courage is the quality
Of mind
That enables a person
To find
His or her strength
At a difficult time
We must be bold
To have our story
Told
To be the example
Of how not to be
Trampled
We must summon
The courage
From Within
To show how
We can win
At any given time.

Crossing the Sea of Suffering

Ship ready to sail
You need a great mast
Standing strong in the center
Dependable and vast
Focused on what could be
In the midst of turbulent seas
Our voyage has begun
No time to hide no time to run
Our course is set
With a keen eye on hope
Holding on to the rope
So tight not to even flinch
In the face of hardships
Believing winning is a cinch
The wind is to our back
Sharing this hope-filled teaching
With courage we don't lack.

Determination

A hope for tomorrow
In all that we do
To make a vow
Make a plan or two
To work together
For the rest of the world
For every man woman
Boy and girl
It's up to us
Me and you
To follow this plan
And see it
Through
Follow your dream
And your hope
For tomorrow
No time to waste
No time to borrow
To have resolve
And not to take lightly
To be involved
Even so slightly
So let us have strong dedication
With our shared cause
Of
Determination.

Don't Take Things Personal

When you have plans
And your plans
Fall through
Don't take things personal.

Things in life
Comes up
So don't hold others
Criminal.

We must learn
Not to treat other
Badly or hold them in contempt.

We must think to ourselves
Something must have happened
Because they had the truest intent.

When dealing with others
We must continue to look inside
Dealing with married men
You must consider his bride.

So when you see me
Please treat me the same
Not like a leper or
Like someone who's untamed.

So when dealing with others
Their response is optional
So to not slander
Don't take things personal.

Dr. Martin Luther King

Let freedom ring
Hated by most
Loved by a few
Stood up against evil
For me and for you
Prayed for
Hatred to cease
As he walked
In peace
Sit-ins at the lunch
Counters
Chased by dogs
Having water hose
Turned on them
beaten and flogged
Tears of sorrow
Tears of pain
to gain equal right
Some were slain
a dark period
In Amerikkka
waiting on light
walked with a smile
didn't even fight
Went to the mountaintop
had a dream
One man made a difference
Dr. Martin Luther King.

Dream as Big as the Universe

Imagine the universe
Large and vast
Creating a future
From the distant past
Believing in self
To its very core
Wide open
Not hiding
Behind a door
Seeing things as it's
Meant to be
Being secure
With security
Goals and dreams
We must add
Write it down
Pen to pad
Like an hourglass
Full of sand
Having big dreams
Big and grand
Not feeling averse
Having a dream
Big as the
Universe.

Emotional Synchronicity

M ight be a mystery to some who do not understand simultaneity.

Some say that it is more than a coincidence to be attached emotionally.

But in truth there is no such thing as coincidence. Everything is causally related.

From the distant past to the closer present this truth has always been orated.

So dry your eyes even when there misty because in truth life is full of emotional synchronicities.

End of the Year

Not a time for screaming
Not a time for neglect
It's a time for dreaming
And a time to reflect
Some people are happy
Some may fear
Not knowing
What tomorrow may bring
Some may cry
Some may sing
Some are looking
Toward the spring
It's a time for change
Time to rearrange
Time to analyze
A time to scan
Time to make
A new plan
So let me be clear
Be of good cheer
Have no fear
And let's keep
Yesterday in the rear
While we work toward
The end of the year.

Equal in Every Way

I think of
How this all began
I think of its true origin
It started centuries ago
At a time when
We were in control
We were kings and queens
That ruled the earth
Now we are hated
From the time of our birth
They came into our society
They plotted and schemed
And brought all kinds of anxiety
They came from miles around
Our kingdoms started tumbling down
Time went by they gained control
They hid the way our story was told
So that we would think
Our story started at the end of a chain link
In truth they were are slaves
In fact while we creating science
They were still in caves
They knew our story more than we did
That is why they kept it hidden
They came and shot the noses
Off stone
But our story had been written

On walls along
Time passed to a future date
Then that fateful day we met our fate
Chains and shackles were our jewelry
They treated us bad and
The treatment was cruelty
Time again passed to a new date in time
We were free but not from their tyranny
They burned our stores and our towns
Because they were jealous of our
Hard work and we still wore our crowns
They used our babies as
Alligator bate but they never
Thought about their fate
Time has passed generations more
A new generation grew
And they burned down their store
Marched in the street in full protest
On how we were treated and not like the rest
Justice for all means justice for me
No more hanging us from an old oak tree
No more police killings, no more not treating us fair
There is a huge shift in the air
Out of the ashes comes a new day
When we all are treated equal in every way.

Expressing Oneself

To express oneself through poetry
Is my relief of anxiety
Thinking of words to say
Just to get me through the day.

I've heard some poems that rhyme
And some that do not
But the poems that rhyme
I think get right to the spot
People express themselves in many forms
no one can say what is the norm
Some people sing some may draw
Some may dance as the ice begins to thaw
But to express oneself is truly noteworthy
That why I express myself through poetry.

Family Harmony

Family harmony
is like a symphony
an orchestra of sounds
of laughter from today
to the hereafter
some families
are estranged
Feelings of
alienation
without an
explanation.
Families are
not a coincidence
predetermined
or a predestined fate
but by a karmic bond
they share the
same
character trait
having an appreciation
toward euphony
is to have
family harmony.

Freedom

To be free means to be in control of self
Words thoughts and deeds
To not be in control feels like you're pulling weeds
Working all day under the hot, hot sun
All work and no play not having any fun
But to be in control feels like a cool summers breeze
Taking responsibility for your life
and living life with ease
Some say that it is easier to blame
others for your pain and trouble
But when you open your hearts and
minds you'll bust your own bubble
So when you stand up and face life
on life's terms with wisdom
You will see how it feels to have true freedom.

From Creation

Looking back on how life used to be
Sixty years young and still have a melody
A song of joy deep in my heart
Looking back seeing it from the start
Skinned knee hurt ego
How it started long time ago
New skills learned badges earned
With the desire for truth and justice always yearned
Eager to try new things
Flying high off of my own wings
Always been the way to go
Even if the wind didn't blow
Standing tall on my own
Couldn't wait to become grown
Growing up was not easy
Not free from pain not for the queasy
hard work and determination
Made me who I am from creation.

Gratitude

What should our attitude be?
In the midst of uncertainty
With distinct clarity
Free from all ambiguity
What actions can we take?
What causes can we make?
To have a clear vision
Of working together
And not of division
We must be able to grasp
That truth that is
Within me and you
By seeing us as the same
Even as equals too
We must not sit in solitude
In a cave far, far away
The key is to be filled
With gratitude
Day after day.

Happiness Means to Me

Happiness means to me
Being in control of my destiny
Control of my ups and downs
Control of my smiles
And my frowns
A choice in what I say
A choice on how
I live my day
Understanding my power within
Understanding what it takes to win
Nothing we can't handle
If we choose
An easy process
We can't loose
Living a trouble-free life
Full of joy and no strife
No doubts in our hearts
Like having a silver spoon
In their mouth
That's what happiness
Means to me.

Happy Holiday

A time for joy
A time for sadness
We can't wait for the end of this madness
A special time of the year
To be close to those that are dear
There will be empty seats at the table
Due to COVID-19 some are not able
To be with the ones they love
Some have left already
And their visions are in the sky above
Cherish the day cherish the year
Live with hope and with good cheer
Say hello to your neighbor's or to a passerby
Smile when you see them and try not to cry
There is light at the end of this long tunnel
Sit back in your small craft and ride on the runnel
Headed to a brighter day when we can all say
Happy holiday!

Head Held High

You're looking for
Answers but don't
Know where to go
Thinking the answer
Is outside
You reap
What you sow
Taking responsibility
For the how and why
You can be happy
Before you die
Words, thoughts, deeds
Karma's plight
Seeing your own
Actions that you can't fight
Life is full
Of amazing things

When your eyes
Are open
Your life
Begins to sing
Songs of joy
Different melodies
Melodic chords
Creating memories
Memories of old
Memories of new
Memories of stories
Some lies some true
But to look inside
And not wonder why
Is the greatest gift
To walk with your
Head held high.

Hope

Hope is a feeling of no despair
You know that feeling like you're floating in air
Hope is a feeling of never giving up
It's like you're finally mature and all grown up
I know that it's hard sometimes to feel hope
But that's the time to feel like you're in a
submarine and raise your periscope.
Looking as far as the eye can see
Wondering how life can truly be
But to know life is to live life and live it full scope
Then you'll understand the true meaning of hope.

Human Right

We must stand for human right
Even if it means we stand and fight
To rid our country of this evil plight
We must keep hope in our sight
Morning noon and night
It's like walking a rope that is pulled real tight.

The conditions in America are really trite
We must come together without a fright
Working for change with all of our might
To see a peaceful world happy and bright
And to respect each person's human rights.

January

Looking back on yesterday
Wondering what might have been
Getting a fresh start
A new determination
Begins
Resolutions
To evolve into someone new
Have direction
Get a clue
Be willing to change
Old habits to new
Work hard
Just and see it through
New goals new dreams
Not as easy task
Be true to ourselves
Remove the Masque
See ourselves
As we are
As if we were
An actuary
Getting ready for
January.

Karma

Karma means action
Words, thoughts, and deeds
We may think that things are a random act
But in truth it's not as it seems
Our karma put hooks into the lives of others
They behave in a way that will
make your life shutter.
We chant to change our past, present, and future
To lessen the effects of our actions
that cause us to suffer
So when we see terrible acts within society
It's just an effect that came back justifiably.

Kosen-rufu

Kosen-rufu is when there is peace
on earth for me and you.
Sharing ideas of joy and laughter
From now until the hereafter
Seeing men woman and youth
working together as one
Enjoying life under the bright morning sun
The daishonin said that nam-myho-renge-
kyo will spread for ten thousand years
Reaping happiness and wiping away those tears.
So I'm doing my part day by day
to change the world too
Just to realize the world of kosen-rufu.

Last throughout Time

Song in our heart
Strikes the perfect key
Finding the right words
With the right melody
Notes on paper
Lines on the staff
Sound so good makes
You want to laugh
Finding the right chord
Major or minor
Bringing it altogether
Makes it much finer
Helping us get out of our seat
The timing of a 4/4 beat
The rhythm of our lives are liken
To a song
We are the conductors of our lives
We can't go wrong
Like a canvass pure and clean
Waiting for the right time
To depict our meme
With the right colors and the right state of mind
We can paint a picture of peace
That last throughout time.

Life's Philosophy

Sharing life's philosophy
Should be as natural as it can be
But talking to people is not as
Easy as it seems
They look at you strange
And wonder what you mean
Especially when you speak of hope
When hope can't be seen
You share heart to heart
From the very start
Because of care and compassion
Trying to make them think
To look at their thoughts
As well as their actions
The object is to plant the seed
By doing this great deed
By putting something
On their mind
Not to confront
Or to put in a bind
We're working for peace
And a world full of harmony
Sharing this great teaching
Life's philosophy.

Living a Life of Gratitude

By living a life of gratitude
There is no regret
Seeing life as it is and not owing a debt
By sharing our joy and our sorrow during the
darkest of times we look forward to tomorrow
Life is full of moments to moments
And time waits for no one
But by living a life of gratitude our
lives shine like the morning's sun
So when things look down and you begin
to have an attitude just remember how
it feels living a life of gratitude.

Mature with Age

Maturing with age is not a
special stage in one's life
Coming into one's own and taking responsibility
when you're full-grown and not full of rife
Maturing comes in stages
And it's not based on ages
It's about being true to oneself
depending on no one else
Maturing is about trials and tribulations
but when you win it's about jubilation
With the understanding that the joy won't
last if you are not steadfast in your deep
belief in self and in no one else.
So as we pull the curtain back on a
different stage we can see and understand
what it means to mature with age.

Me or You

Businesses are closed
No food on the table
People trying to get by
But they're not able
Some are sick
Some are going to be
They're trying to open
The state in the mist
Of this catastrophe
Opening the state
On the first of May
Not caring what
The experts say
Wash your hands
Twenty seconds or more
Stand six feet away
While you're at the
Grocery store
Economy is a must
For his election sake
No time to test
Just money to make
More people may die
Not just a few
I'm just hoping
It's not
Me or You.

Memoriam

In memory of those who made
the greatest sacrifice
We honor you on this day not thinking twice
You're bravery and courage gave so much hope
You took away their fear and helped them cope
So to the brave men and women
of the armed services
We thank you for your courage and dedication
You served with honor without hesitation
You made your parents and relatives proud
Giving up was not an option the
thought was not allowed.
So one this day we salute you too
For your service and for all that you do.

Mirror, Mirror

Mirror, mirror on the wall
How can I be happy once and for all?
Looking at others but not seeing me
Is the greatest evil and the worst tragedy
Thinking that they should comply with my wishes
Is not believing in their worth and it dismisses
Their unique ability to be who they are
Not what I think which can be subpar
Happiness starts from within
Not where some think it begin
Outside of ourselves someone else is to blame
By giving that power to others make us lame
Be strong be bold someone once said
Be who you are and don't be led
Acknowledge the power within
And you can see how you can win
Have no doubt in the power of self
True happiness comes from nowhere else
It starts from the bottom of our feet
To the top of our head
Being happy in life not living like we're dead
Head held high walking straight and tall
We can smile while were looking
At the mirror, mirror on the wall.

Mother's Day Poem

I'm sitting here trying to think of the words to say to all the moms on Mother's Day.

You are there for us in many ways throughout our lives on many days

You stood by us when no one else would give us your love the best that you could.

You should be cherished and appreciated throughout the year because you are special you can take away our fear

But today is set aside for you as a special day so that we can shower you with gifts of love on Mother's Day.

Happy Mother's Day to all.

Mothers of Soka

M others of Soka are full of grace
They work really hard to make this a peaceful place
Mothers of Soka are really dedicated to the cause
They work very hard not looking for applause
They will travel day and night
Just to give hope and to help us rid our plight
So thank you to the mothers of Soka one and all
For helping the rest of us stand and not fall.

Never Give Up

When the sky grows dark and
the storms begin to flow
Never give up
Keep your head held high and not down low
Never give up
We must summon the strength from within
We must fight from beginning to end
Never give up
Life is filled with joy and sorrow
But by never giving up we can
look forward to tomorrow.

You're Not Alone

We are not together
In a physical sense
Through chanting
We are connected
And the light is not dense
The power to unite
Is infinitely profound
We still have unity
Even when no one's around
The unity that we share
Is special and true
There's a connection
Between me and you
Some may call
Some may text
Some may not
Don't be vexed
Apple, peaches, pears
Come from a different root
They're all different
But they're all fruit
Like a rock in the ocean
Become a large stone
Please remember
We're united together
You're not alone.

Our Only Salvation

In a world full of confusion
We come to one conclusion
There is only one solution
Hearing lies being told
Not from the weak
But from the bold
Every day new books
Are being sold
But there is hope
In the scope
To help us cope
By having someone to
Show us the way
How to live our lives
Each and every day
Being that example for us to see
Caring for you and for me
Being of the same mind
Showing care and being kind
But in a world full of confusion
We come to one conclusion
There is only one solution
We must use critical thought
Fight against the onslaught
Of lies and vilification
Believing in power of self
Is our only salvation.

Our Story

From the Nile Valley
To Timbuktu
They came to learn math, science
And astronomy too
They broke the nose
Off of histories past
Trying to hide our story
To create a new caste
Wise ones knew that
Day would come
So they told our story
On stone columns
They wrote on walls
All over the land
To tell our story
Of power and grand
We were kings and queens
As far back as the mind can see
We ruled the earth
For twenty-four dynasties
Remember the facts
How our story was told
We predated slavery
From days of old.

Peace of Mind

In a world full of confusion there is only one
solution and one conclusion is to have a peace of
mind

We are hearing lies being told not from the weak but
from the bold
Every day new books are being sold

We must use critical thought to fight against the
onslaught of lies and vilification

Every day there is something new and some things
that are being told untrue about the humankind

But to see the truth in all things
Is when you have a true peace of mind.

People of Compassion

People of compassion will
Tell the truth no matter
How one may feel
It will be honest
Straight from the heart
And it would
Most definitely be real.
People who lack
Courage and compassion
Tell you what they
Think you want to hear
They'll smile on your face
But they are
Acting out of fear
They will pat you on your back
And send you on your way
Not really caring how you feel
Or what you have to say
Stop and think of how someone else may feel
Being kind and caring makes it feel real
Proof is in the action
Of people of compassion.

World's Fate

Please check my elocution
In a world full of confusion
We must come up with a solution
To end all of this delusion.

It's an illusion
To think that we must have seclusion
But in fact we must have inclusion.

To keep people apart
Is only the start
Of the world not having a heart.

We don't look or sound the same
But everyone is pointing at others
instead of self taking the blame
And it's a damn shame.

So let's stand up against hate
Let's not take the bait
We're responsible for the world's fate.

Possibilities of Tomorrow

Love, peace, joy, and happiness
Are words that express
Hope in order to cope
With the lies being told
And the manipulation of the bold
To the people who seek
A better life each and every week
To grasp and get a grip
On life's fleeting tip
Trying to hold on to the norm
From the darkest of night
To the glow of the sun in the morn
Each and every day we're dealing with life
On life's terms in every way
Understanding what we have learned
Striving to yearn for the possibilities of
Tomorrow.

Power in You

Not believing in self
Is the greatest of all sin
Having untold power
Not knowing it comes from within
Like reading a book like a fairy tale
Big black stallion with a long black tail
Galloping fast over a long distance
Unable able to see not even a glance
Believing in luck and even chance
We must teach our youth
How to reach their dream
Yes, life sometimes makes you want to scream
The object is not to give up
Nor to give in
All we need is a plan and
determination to see it through
Believe in the power in you.

Power of the Heart

The power of the heart
Is where to start
When things begin
To look gloomy and dark.

Some say that the
Heart is the same
As the mind
But it's something
That doesn't bind.

The power of the heart
Shouldn't fluctuate
It should actuate
Keep things moving
And in line.

So when you're lost
And full of no hope
Change your determination
And change your scope.

Make a vow
And look deep, deep inside
To change your circumstances
No matter how wide.

We have the power to see
What we want our life to be
So let's do our part
And create the
Power of the heart.

Respecting Others

Respecting others should be a trait that we learned from our mothers

To treat one with disdain
Is wrong we should treat everyone with the same refrain.

No one is better than others but to treat someone with disrespect should make all our hearts shutter.

So before you interrupt someone and make them feel disrespected,
You should stop and think about how it would make you feel being neglected.

Seasons

In the skyway above the earth
Seasons take their form
From hot sunny days
To a cold winter storm
Winter boots and overcoats
Are clothing that we wear
Leaves from the tree's
All die
Leaving the tree's all bare
The trees are all asleep
Waiting for new birth
The grass is turning green
Growing from within the earth
Spring brings showers
Flowers begin
To bloom
Then there's fall
Which seem to always
Come too soon
There is birth and rebirth
Spreading across the land
Like a well-seasoned steak
Seasoned and not bland
Different dates different climates
All are not wizen
But that special time
Is called
A season.

Seeing Ourselves

Seeing ourselves in others eyes
Seeing ourselves in other's eyes
Can be a shock even a great surprise
It is our responsibility
To show with our lives
Our respectability
We say this, we say that
But it's actually us
Underneath that hat
So what matters most
Is how to improve
Make better
How to get our groove
So we create value
Only with a smile
By saying hello
Even if we feel
Were on trial
And when we do
Others will be surprised
Especially when we see ourselves in other's eyes.

Special Way

Today was a very
Special day
I received many
Calls and texts
Just to say
Hey bro
I'm thinking of you
And I just had to say
Happy birthday
So in my own way
I too would like to say
To you one and all
With this little poem
Thank you
You all made my day
In your own special way.

Success

Some say that success is power and fame but true success is not blaming others but taking the blame.

The secret to success is not giving up
But working hard on ourselves
To become mature and growing up.

By looking straight into the mirror and not leaving our responsibilities on top of shelves we can be free and jump for joy like a gazelle.

So let's not digress but let's continue showing positive results
Towards our future and toward our progress of
Being successful adults.

Summertime

Summertime is a time for a cool glass of lemonade
Laying quietly in the shade
A time for family cookouts and parades
Playing cards and playing charades.
Watching children playing in the park
all day and late until after dark.
These are the times to cherish to
make memories young and old
To sit by a fire listening to stories being told
Enjoy your summer one and all because living
here in Cleveland it will soon be fall.

A Must

Technicalities physicality's
Choices that we choose
Nothing to write home about
Just a formality to loose
Being at one place
Or being at two
Ultimately it's your decision
And all it's up to you
Consistency and uniformity
Are key
Dependability is worthy
Of trust
Reliability is a staple
And a must.

The District

The district is
Like a service station
The best location
To check under the hood
Making sure all levels are good
A place to clean the glass
And to get more gas
Especially when you're not on full
A place to energize
To polish our magnificent jewel
With encouraging words
From friends and strangers
Keeping us on the right path
And out of danger
We come once a week
Listening to others speak
Sharing joys and sorrow's
Getting much-needed encouragement
To look forward to our tomorrow's
district.

The Right Attitude

What should our attitude be
In the midst of uncertainty?

With distinct clarity
Free from all ambiguity

What actions can we take?
What causes can we make?

To have a clear vision
Of working together
And not of division

We must be able to grasp
That truth that is within me and you
By seeing us as the same
Even as equals too.

We must not sit in solitude
In a cave far, far away
The key is to be filled with gratitude
Day after day.

The Sky Is Not Falling

Fear is in the air
From the city streets
To the county fair
Long lines at the store
People sleeping at grocer's door
Waiting to buy toilet paper
From the two-bedroom house
To the large skyscraper
People staying home
Some will be alone
Because of fear
Panic, panic
Is everywhere
On all the TV channels
And on cable news
But fear is something I refuse
To choose
If I'm to be sick
Let it be

If I am it was meant to be
I can't waste my time
Wondering what if
If you're that scared
Jump off a cliff
Wash your hands
And keep them from
Your face
Use hand cleaner and towels
And wipe up the place
Tomorrow was never promised
To anyone
It's a gift to
Wake and see the sun
So have a goodnight
And sleep real tight
And try not to be bawling
Because the sky is
Not falling.

The Universe Is Listening

When your thoughts are running
A mile a minute
Feels like a strange world
And you're not in it
Wondering if someone really cares
Wondering if you can really dare
To dream the impossible dream
Dreams of hope dreams of laughter
Working for today and the day after
Working for a brighter day
Hoping our fears will run far away
Wanting to see peace
Happiness for you and for me
Hope is in your eyes and your eyes are glistening
Don't give up because
The universe is listening.

Ticktock

Ticktock
Goes the hands
Of the clock
Spring forward
Fall back
How can we
See ourselves
On our behavior
Or what we lack
Looking in our mirror
And seeing what
We see
Is how we
Reflect
On how
We should be

Time waits for
No one
Time does not
Standstill
It's up to us
To continue
To grow
And to learn
Life's skill
It's like
Bringing a ship
To dock
Listening to a clock
Go ticktock
Ticktock.

Today We Honor Dad

The one who's misunderstood
The one who's not around sometimes as he should

Sometimes in life things happen and he's not around
But it doesn't mean he doesn't care it just means he
searches for the right words but they can't be found

Society has him in a round box
They see him as threat to their false paradox

But without him we wouldn't be alive today
So on this day we say Happy Father's Day.

Unity

U nity is when
We come together
In any type of weather
For a goal or a plan
Each person
Playing their role
To achieve a specific goal
To help their
Fellow man
We have been
Unified for so long
It seems natural
To sing our own song
But with the right
Melody in the right key
We can come together
Once again for
Unity.

Value

Some say diamonds
Are of value
Golds are of value too
Working towards
Peace
is something
That we all can do
Human beings
Has a choice
In how we should live
We have a choice in
What we can give
Let give hope
And let's give good cheer
Let's stay on course
And be focused
And do not veer
The road to happiness
Is not as far as we think
Is true
But with the right effort
We can create
Value.

Glass Ceiling

A new day of hope
Is beyond the scope
Of someone that can't cope
With life's daily challenges
Obstacles and challenges are there for us
To change ourselves from our muss
In an age of uncertainty with no direction
With hope, determination and self-reflection
We can make a difference that we can see
We can be the humans that we are meant to be
Courage is key in the mist of adversity
Follow my words with a close ear
Remove your doubt and remove your fear
Look toward tomorrow with a fresh feeling
Like rising up and breaking that glass ceiling.

When Will It End

Fighting for human rights
Fighting with all our might
To be equal as one
To be free
From rivers to the sea
Creating peace
Wishing for the violence to cease
Weapons in their hand
All across the land
People being killed
Not protected
By the shield
So many people dying
So many people crying
Protesting having something to say
Praying for a new day
Unable to hide
The pride inside
Making a vow
A determination
To win
We keep asking our selves
When will it end?

Who We Were Meant to Be

Faith is nothing new or extraordinary
It is a belief in self and that's what's necessary.
Without faith in self is like dish that is
not seasoned and its taste is bland
It's like walking blindly and falling in quicksand.
We must summon up courage each and every
day to walk through life in an enlightened way.
We must demonstrate our faith in
our words thoughts and deed
We must continue to chant and to continue to read
The daishonin said that people in
his land is happy and free
Through study helps us become
who we were meant to be.

Why

Why is it that no one helps
Those that are weak?
They rather look the other way
And not even speak.

They rather close one's ears
And hide one's eyes.
They rather walk away
When a baby cries.

Why do we accept
The status quo
Instead of making a change
To help others grow?

The world today is full of
Sorrow and pain.
People are just looking
For what they can gain.

So I ask this question
Over and over again
What can I do?
Where to begin?

Where can I start?
How can I try?
And I found the answer
First is to ask why.

Winner in Life

It has been said
Life as a human
Is hard to sustain.

Like morning dew
On grass that doesn't remain.

We must live our lives
With honor day by day.

By watching what we
Think and by watching
What we say.

We must be an example
For all to see
As a shining example
Of our humanity.

So let us be better than
We were yesterday
With all our tomorrows
Full of rife.

To be that example
Of a winner in life.

Winter Turns to Spring

Spring is in the air
How refreshing spring will be
Flowers bloom plants grow
thanks to the bumble bee
April showers come pouring down
With the tat tat tat sound on the ground
Days are longer with the sun up high
Beams of rays illuminating from the sky
Shining bright on you and me
How wonderful life can truly be
Seeing life through a different lens
Makes you stop and wonder how'd this begin
Being able to understand
We are all equal woman and man
With all the obstacles we humans face
It's not difficult to finish the race
All we need is to determine to win
Because winter turns to spring.

The World Is in Turmoil

Corruption is at an all-time high
People are talking but it's mostly lies, hands
up, don't shoot hands, raised to the sky
Can't breathe, get off my neck, when are our
bad cops going to be held for their neglect?
People want to live they don't want to die
When is the government going
to hear the people's cry?
COVID-19 is in the air and on the surfaces to
Masking up protects me and protects you
Praying for a new day to come
No place to hide no place to run
Stand up straight have faith
And don't recoil
Faith is what the world needs today
because the world is in turmoil.

The Face of My Ancestor

Looking in the mirror and who do I see
In the reflection looking back at me
Through pain and grace
It's all across my face
Lines in my forehead to the lines in my chin
Is the look of someone determined to win
Fighting with all of my might
Against all evil and its plight
The gaze in my eyes is no surprise
The glide in my step is really hep
From days of old
Thoughts and words can be oh so bold
With that gaze that could also be so cold
Just like Nestor it's
The face of my ancestor.

A New Day Begin

Woke up and looked out of the window
Wondering where did the time go
Time seems to fly right by
Not a cloud in the sky
The sky is shiny and bright
The moon was shining last night
Arose with new hopes and new dreams
Knowing life is not as it seems
With the right frame of mind
We can conquer our thoughts
So that it will be sublime
Focusing on the here and now
Working for change with a sacred vow
Is how we will win again and again
When we arise and a new day begin.

Always by Our Side

Woke up this morning in the new day sun
Overcame many obstacles
Don't know how I've won
Make the impossible possible
Is what they say
Change your words, thoughts and
actions for a better way
Like a new life
Suckling and didn't know why
Believed in the Gosho so I gave it a try
Gosho's are teachings of old
Followed instructions as they were told
Life is not easy but we have a plan
Don't take it lightly don't just scan
Use the map of life as our guide
Because the Daishonin and Sensei
is always by our side.

We Are All Equal

Looking at life in a different way
Yesterday tomorrow and even today
Seeing it as it really is
Like a thought that just flew by like a whiz
To see with an eye of an eagle
Believing our lives are rich and regal
Like a golfer's game that's above par
We are more than we think we are
To walk through life with a different view
Is a thought and action that we choose
Choice is an option that we all possess
To be able to see life differently
begins with a process
Life is like a good book with a sequel
You can read between the lines and
see that we are all equal.

Again

In a world full of possibilities
There are no mysteries
What we can accomplish
Without any anguish
It's likened to a dream
Floating down stream
On a cool summer night
Knowing everything will be alright
Next day in the morning light
Take a chance is what they say
Everything will be ok
Take that leap of faith
And don't be frightened by a wraith
Be bold be bold be bold
Let your story be told
Of how you won and didn't give in
When you win again and again.

Perfect Enlightenment

To have a situation and comprehend
Is to see it from the beginning to the end
Not on a superficial level or on a shallow plain
But to understand the dominating power
Of how the law of life reign
The law is perfect and has no flaws
We can see the effect and we can see the cause
Karma is action in all that we do
It affects me and affects you too
From the mountain top to the valley below
It's the same yesterday today and tomorrow
There is no escape from the power within
It's up to you to have a desire to win
Win over self is the key
To avoid being helpless and being in misery
With determination and not a
sense of bewilderment
We will eventually gain the power
of perfect enlightenment.

Heart of Self

Happiness is not the easy things of everyday
It's the difficult obstacles that come our way
It's relative and absolute
How we view our circumstance must be resolute
To view life in a positive way
Is how to get through life everyday
We must check our words thoughts and deeds
In order for us to succeed
In a world full of pain and doubt
We must be strong
As we grow and our confidence sprout
Sprout like a tree healthy and strong
Believing in self we can't go wrong
Happiness can't be found anywhere else
It's found deep down in the heart of self.

Change You Wish to See

In the midst of an incredible scene
We can all still achieve our dreams
By setting goals and seeing it through
Working hard and being honest too
Make a plan and write it down
Make a smile from a frown
Believe in the power of you
And your dreams will eventually come true
It may not be today may not be tomorrow
Whenever it comes there will be no sorrow
Life will change to what it's supposed to be
When you be the change that you wish to see.

Best That You Can

It's that time again
the end of the year
We concurred many problems
With hope and not with fear
As we look back and take an overview
We can view ourselves true and anew
Challenges are the fuel to help us grow
Seeing and believing is how we know
So set a goal and make a plan
Don't hold any doubts
And do the best that you can.

What's Right

Saying hello and how do you do
The polite way to speak and be spoken too
Being human in every way
Is what this world needs especially today
Being kind with compassion
Others will respond in kind to your action
We mustn't have hatred or contempt
With the law of cause and effect no one is exempt
You reap what you sow in every way
It's best to be kind
So that kindness will come your way
Have a big smile and be of good cheer
We affect those around us and those who are near
It's sad that some don't believe that this is true
Just look at their actions they don't have a clue
Blaming the world for how they feel
Not believing that its themselves that's real
Be that beacon that guiding light
With your example you can
demonstrate what's right.

Human Revolution

Changing oneself is not an easy task
We carry karma from our distant past
Karma is action in all that we do
Walk talk and even our thoughts too
Change your habits some might say
When you change you'll be able to
see life in a brand-new way
Being aware is the key you'll look at life
Not as a mystery
Focus on the positive and on the good
Live our lives like humans as we should
Not hating our neighbors when they come around
See the positive in them from their head
To their feet firm on the ground
Not with our head high in the clouds
But standing straight and not like the crowd
With all that is said looking for a solution
There's only one way
through having a human revolution.

When You Win

Having hope in the 21st century
Shouldn't be shrouded by a deep mystery
It has been shared for over 60 years
How to find hope and defeat our fears
From the north south east and west
Some of the entire world and parts of the rest
Finding hope hidden deep inside
Letting go of ego and swallowing pride
Seeing others as I see you
Having faith in me and me in you too
That's the beginning of a better day
To walk by faith is what they say
Having a hope in all that we do
Having a choice and seeing it through
That's the start beginning and end
To complete the race and come in first
When you win.

Treasures of the Heart

Creating a life full of life
Is meant to be a life free of strife
We have a choice in all that we do
How I'm treated and how I treat you
Some think treasures are diamonds and gold
It's to care for others without being told
Showing compassion and that you care
Helps those who are suffering
and living a nightmare
To care for others is an act of faith
It's a choice that should not be haith
Making a strong oath with a determined vow
Is something we can do right here and now
Caring for others from the very start
Is to believe in the power of the
treasures of the heart.

Without Misery

Planting the seed of understanding
One seed at a time
Not being too demanding
It will grow into its prime
Enlightenment grows as it matures
Some days it feels like you're unsure
You are never too young or never too old
Even in the midst of the bitter cold
To nourish the seed
In order to succeed
Searching for understanding
Like a plane coming in for a landing
The ground does not need to be smooth
With the knowledge that you can use
Gaining power that you can see
Is living life without misery.

Be Bold

Never give up never surrender
Keep on fighting no matter what's your gender
Don't give up on your hopes
Don't give up on your dreams
Don't hold any doubts
And you'll see what I mean
Life has struggles to make us strong
By believing in ourselves we can't go wrong
Challenging ourselves is our greatest feat
When you rise up to the challenge you can be beat
Keep your head held high in the darkest of times
Remember this poem remember this rhyme
Keep pushing forward with a positive attitude
In the realm of faith become one of certitude
Be certain be sure of the power that you hold
Walk straight and tall and be bold be bold be bold.

2021

The year of hope and victory
A life not full of misery
A triumph over the enemy within
Fighting valiantly trying to win
Win over ourselves, our doubts
Our confusion
Seeing ourselves true without any illusions
Fighting for the greater self to shine through
Working for peace in all that we do
Believing that we can change
We can rearrange
We can alter our thoughts
And our actions
Not falling prey to detraction
Being as happy as the sun in 2021.

About the Author

Howard Churchwell is a husband, father of three and grandfather of ten, musician, and bandleader in Cleveland, Ohio. He enjoys the serenity of writing poetry and encouraging others daily. Howard also likes a good movie, a movie in which he can connect with the actor on an emotional level.